SPHERE

First published in Great Britain in 2016 by Sphere

10 9 8 7 6 5 4 3 2 1

A CIP catalogue record for this book is available from the
British Library.

ISBN 978-0-7515-6633-8

Printed in Italy

Sphere
An imprint of
Little, Brown Book Group
Carmelite House
50 Victoria Embankment
London EC4Y 0DZ

An Hachette UK Company
www.hachette.co.uk

www.littlebrown.co.uk

The Candy Crush Soda Colouring Book

Creatively Colour the Candy Kingdom

sphere

Set in the magical world of the Candy Kingdom, Candy Crush Soda introduces us to sisters Kimmy and Tiffi, and to best friend Yeti, whose home is in the Chocolate Mountains.

Sublime!

The sodalicious Candy Kingdom features *Stickylicious* landscapes, *Juicy* patterns and *Sweet* shapes. All you need are pens, pencils and a bit of imagination to bring the mouth-watering world of Candy Crush Soda to life!

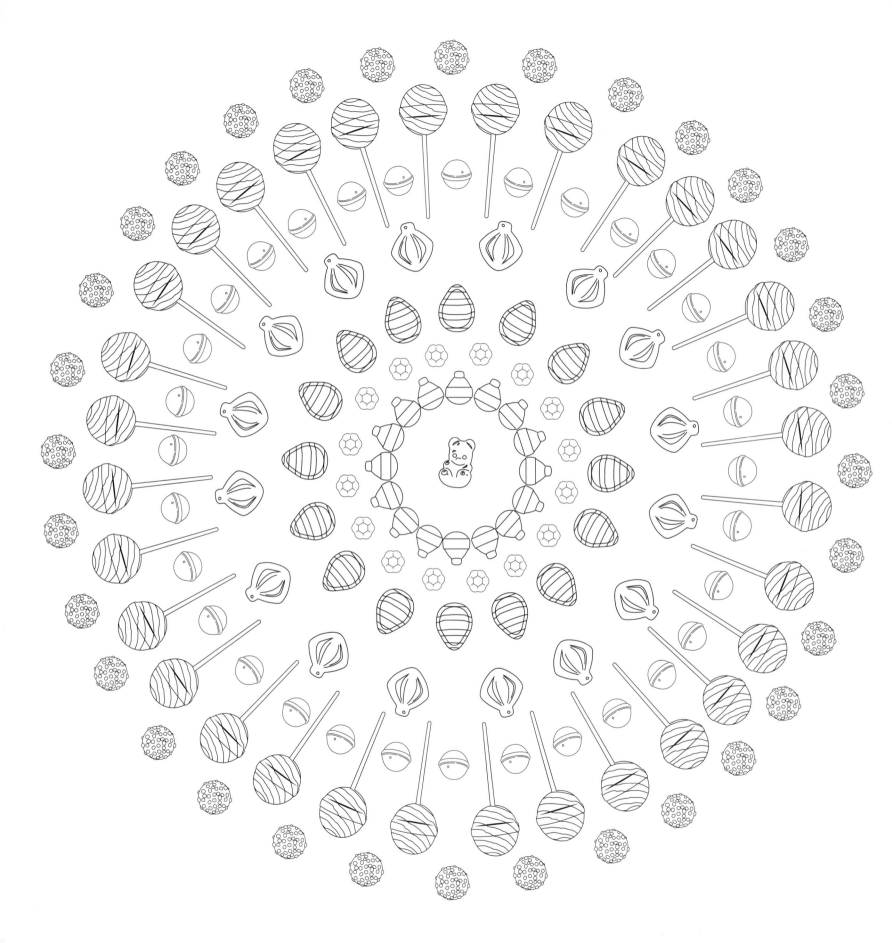

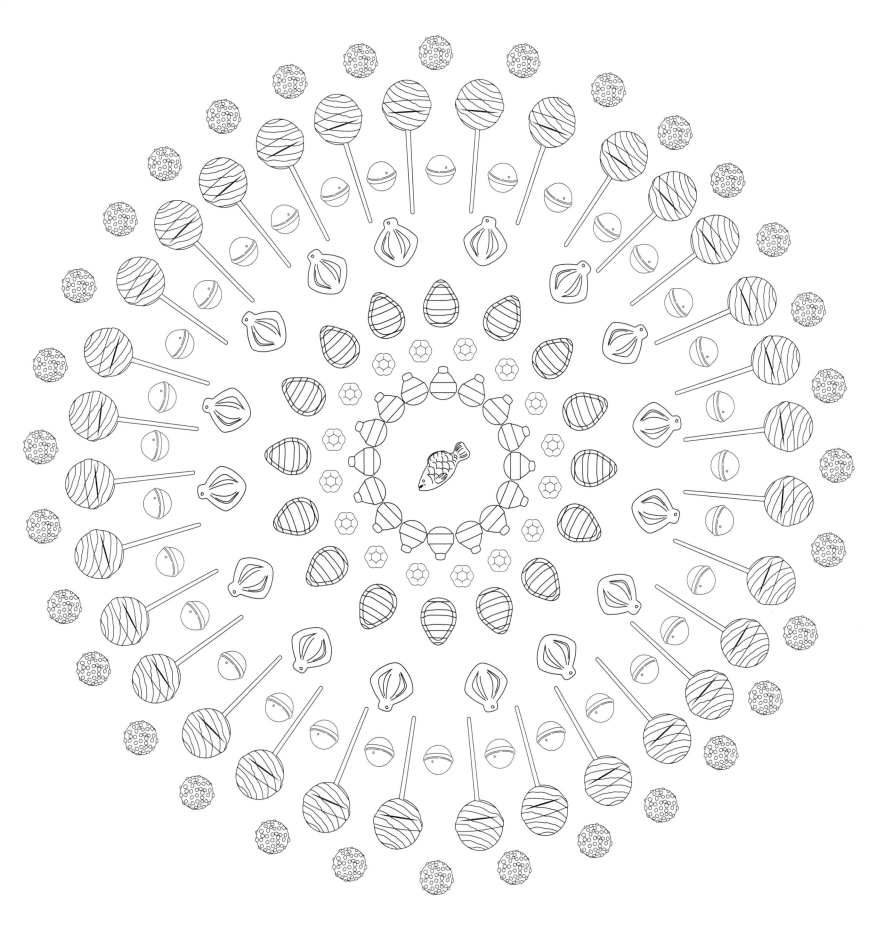

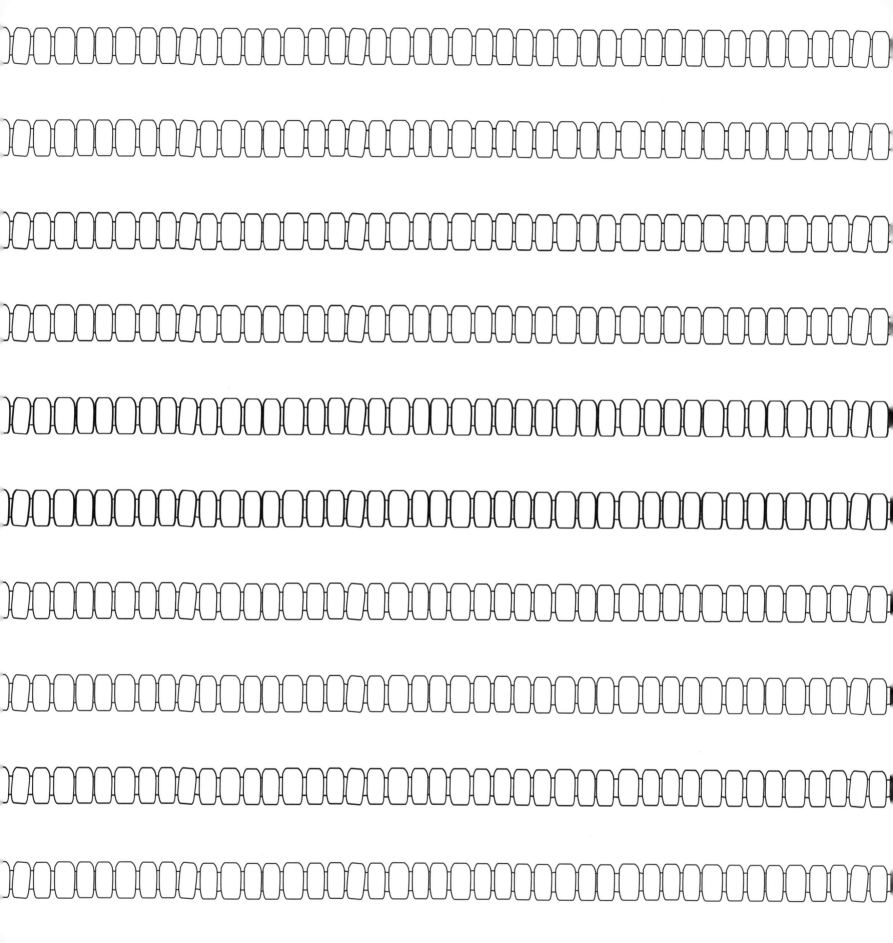

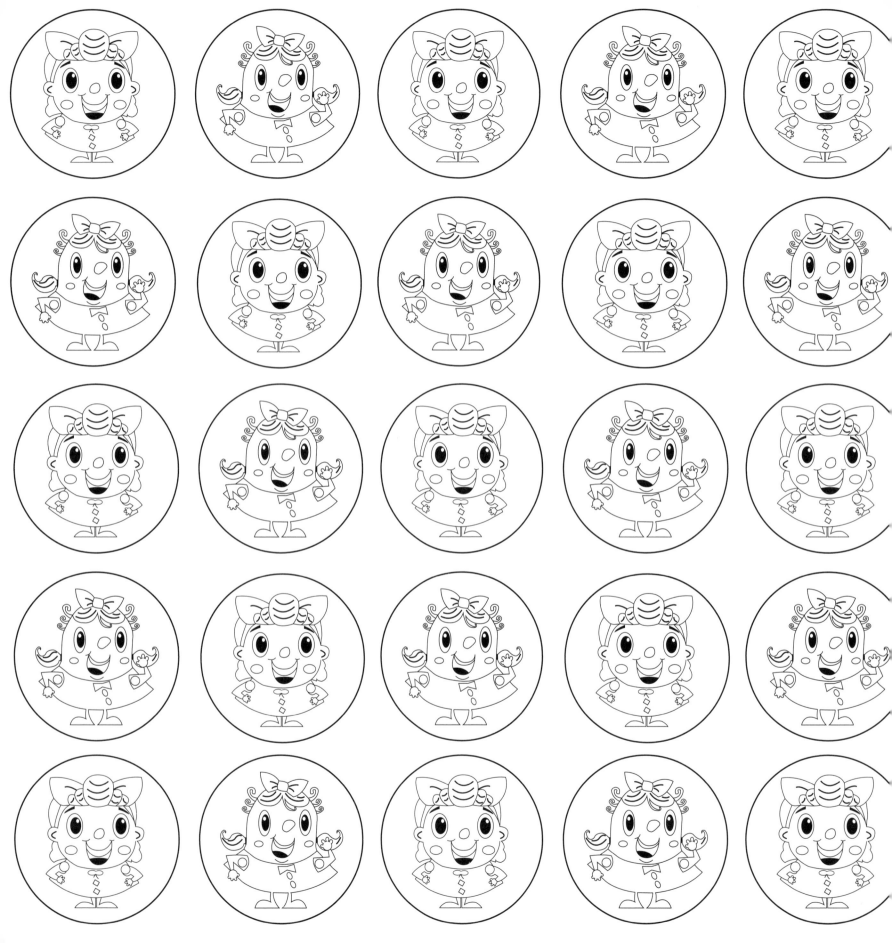

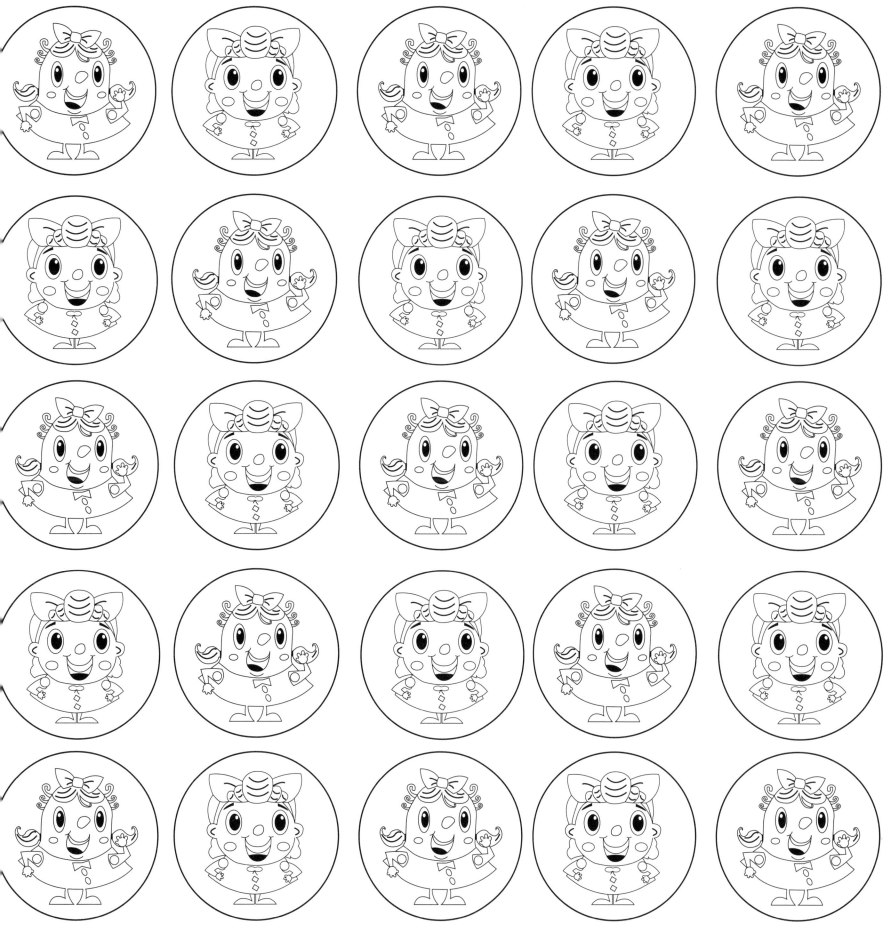

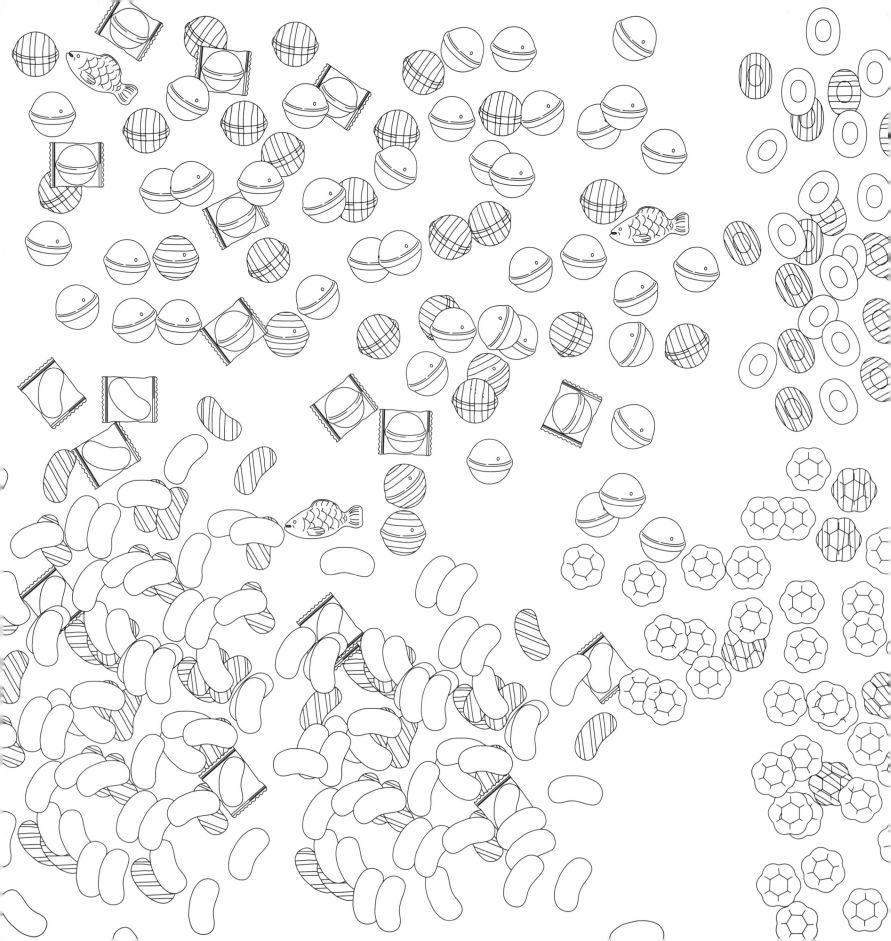

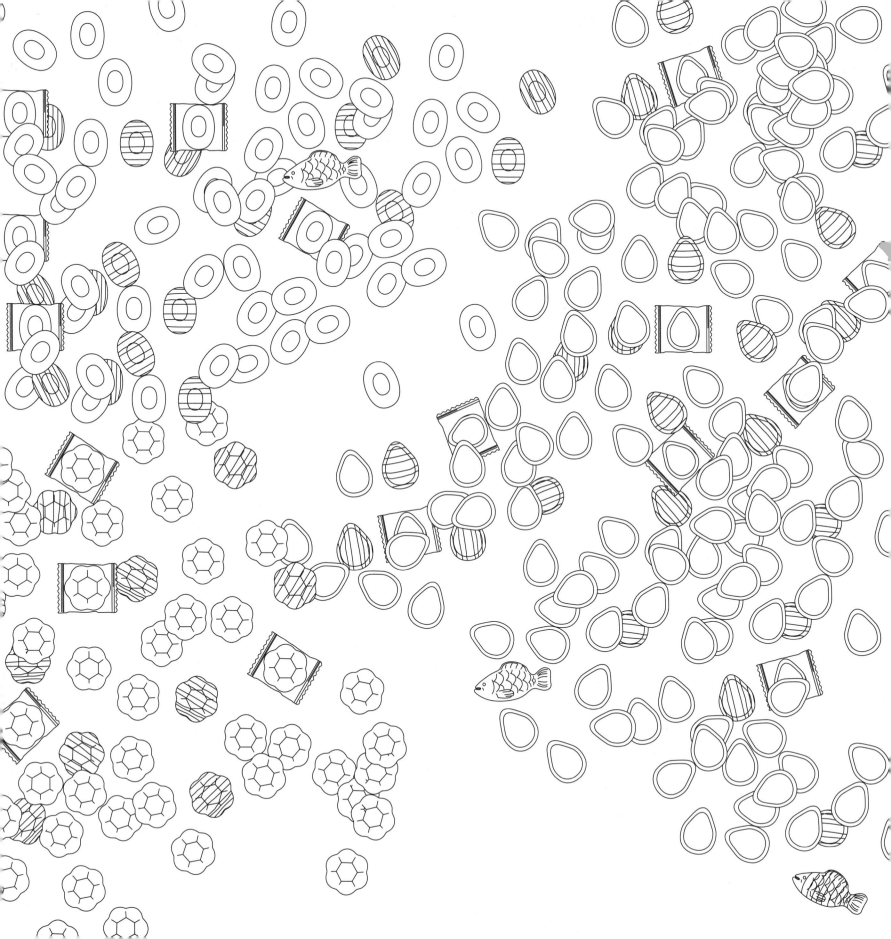

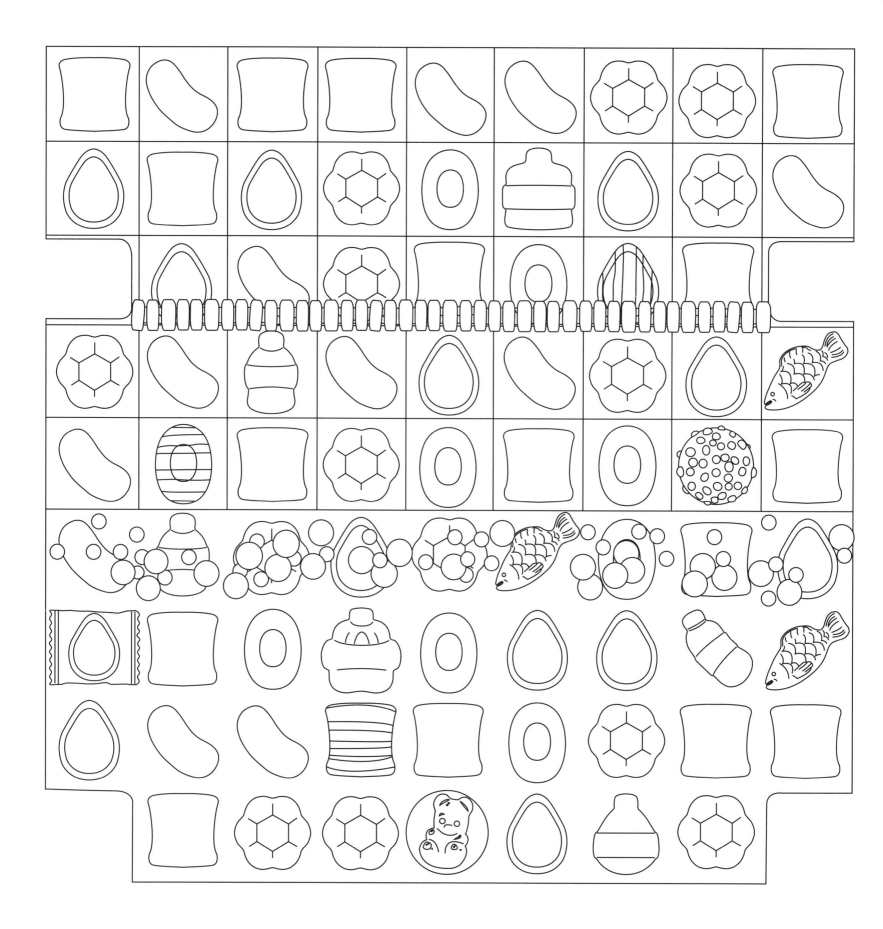

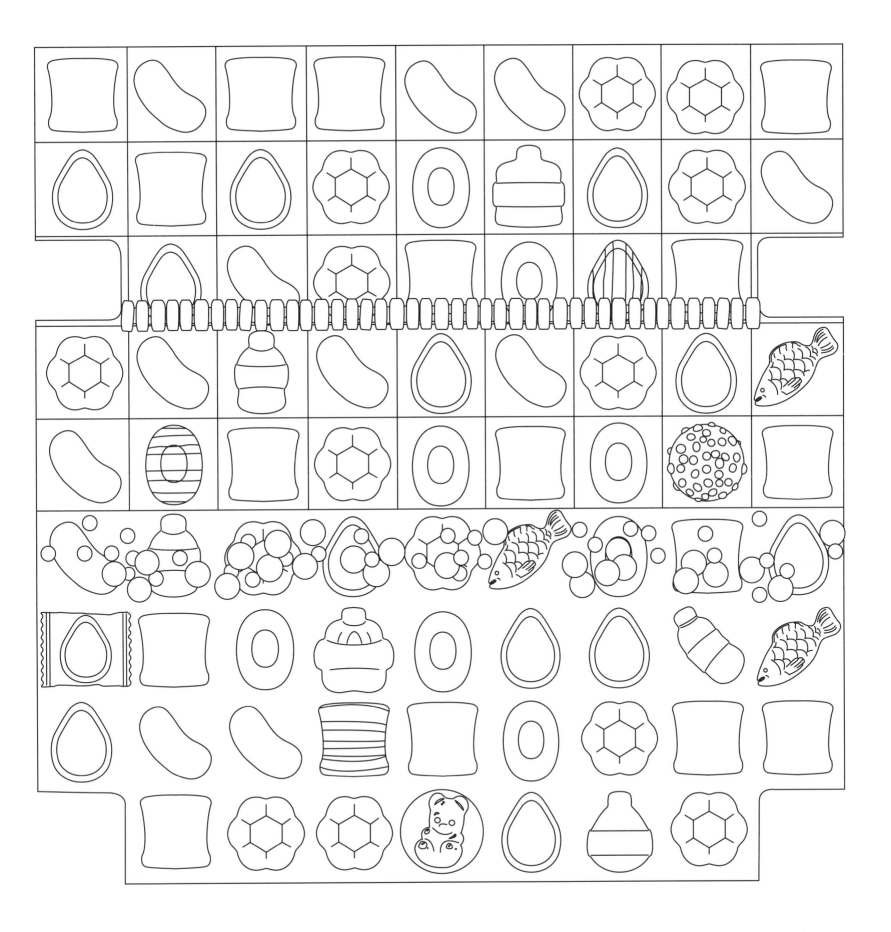

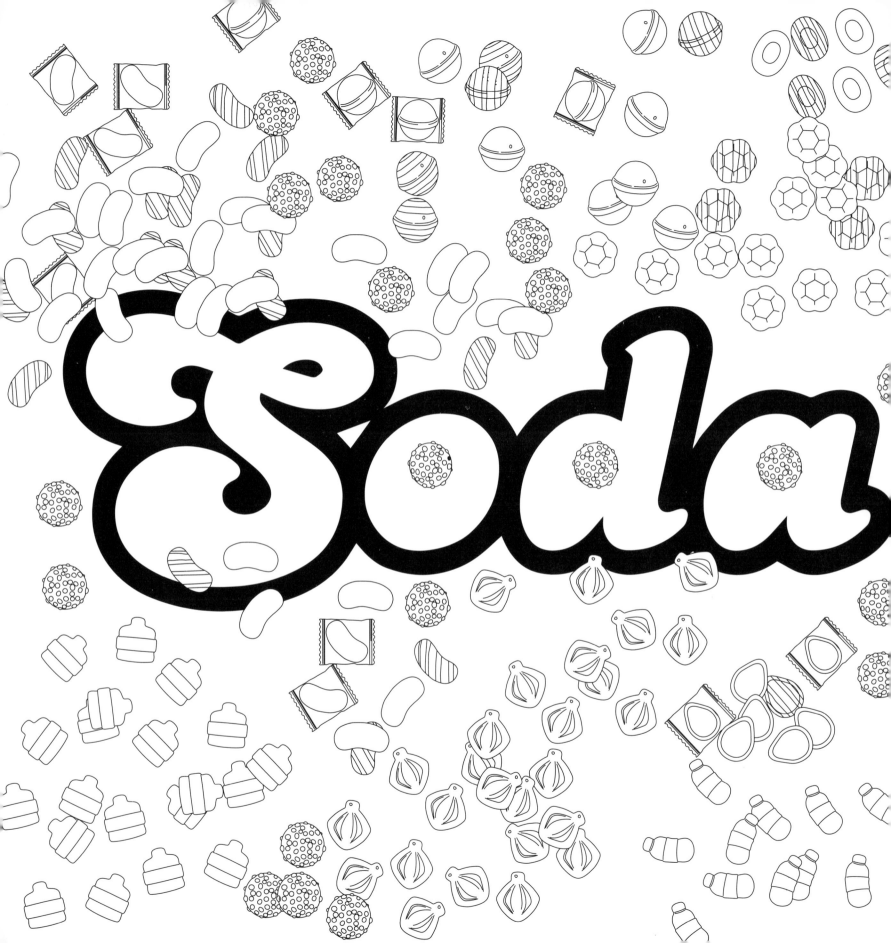

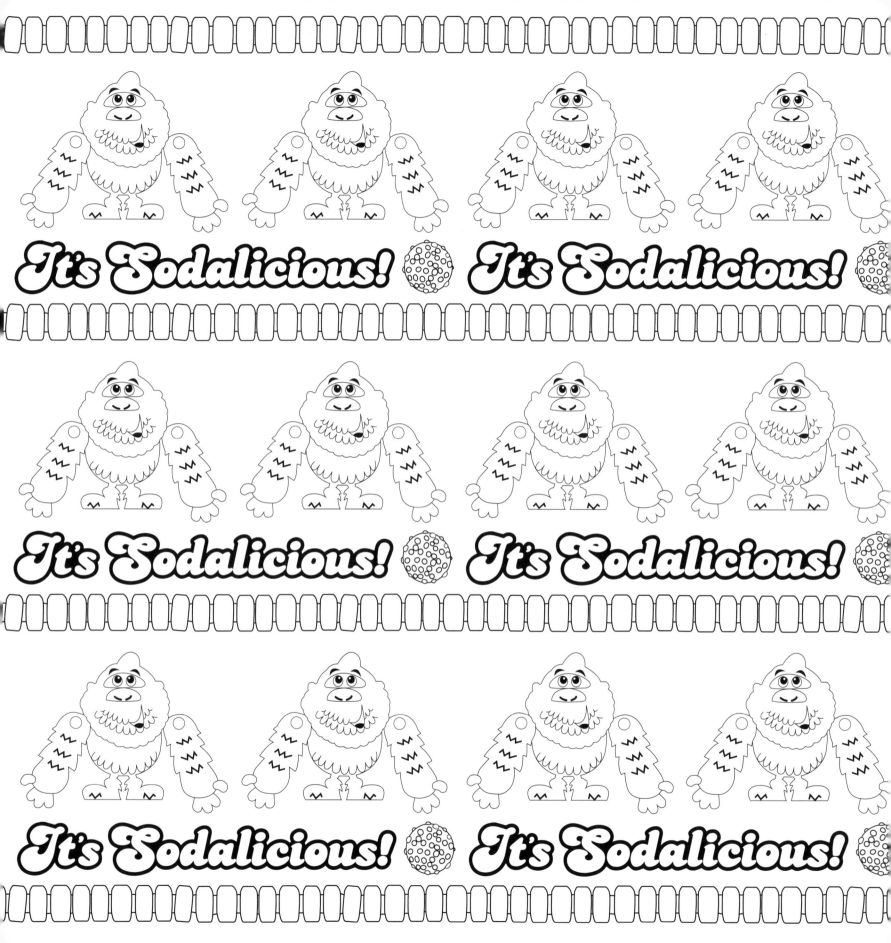

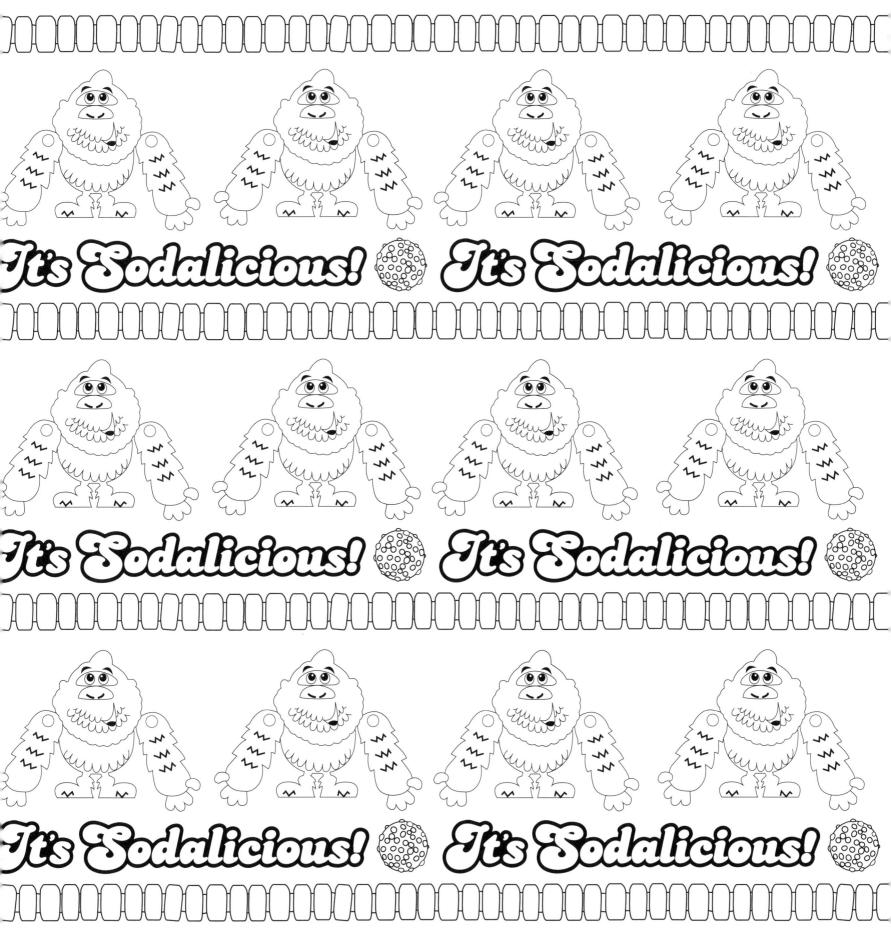

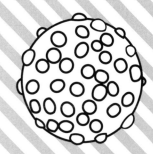

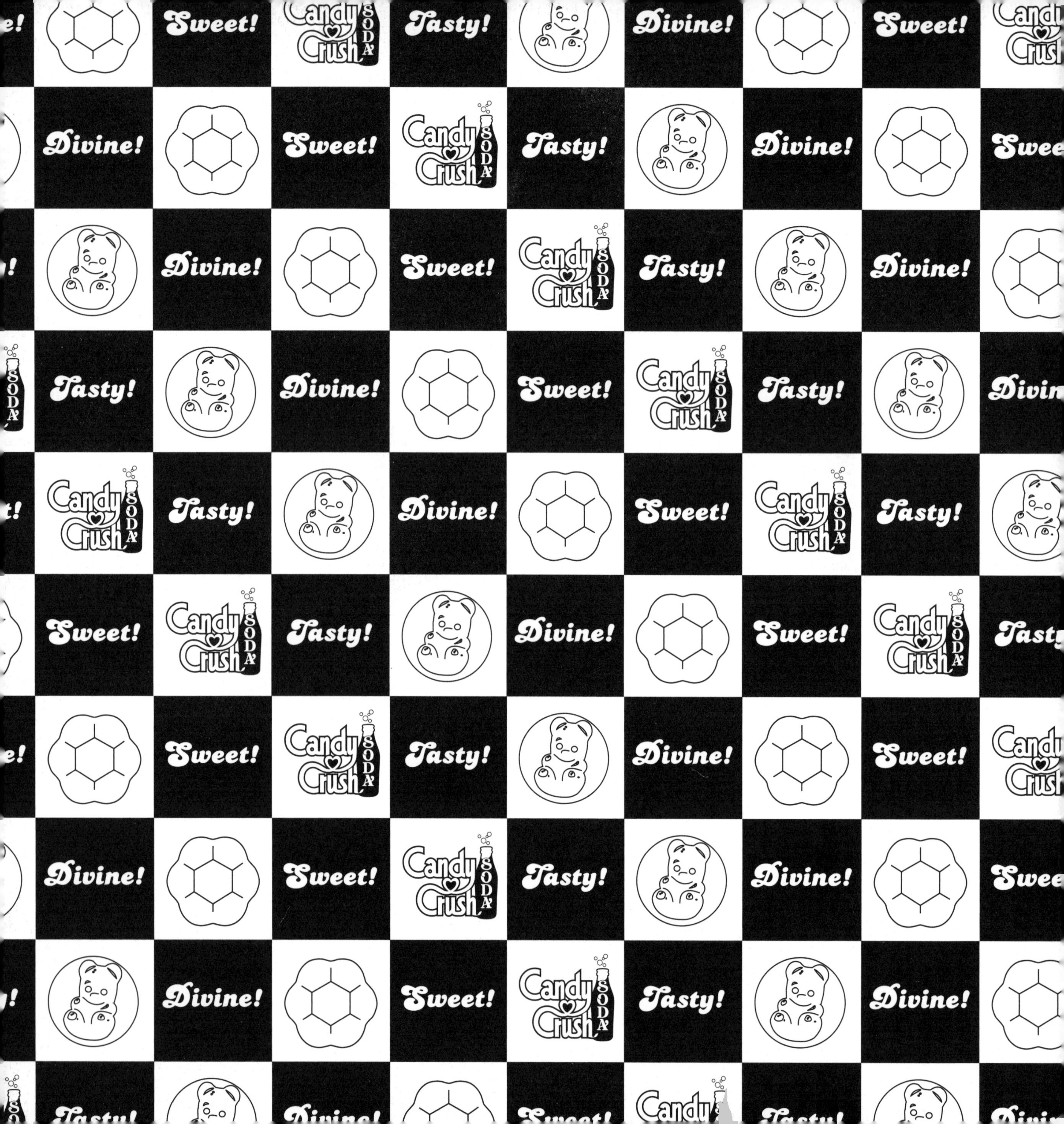
Sweet!
Tasty!
Divine!
Candy Crush SODA

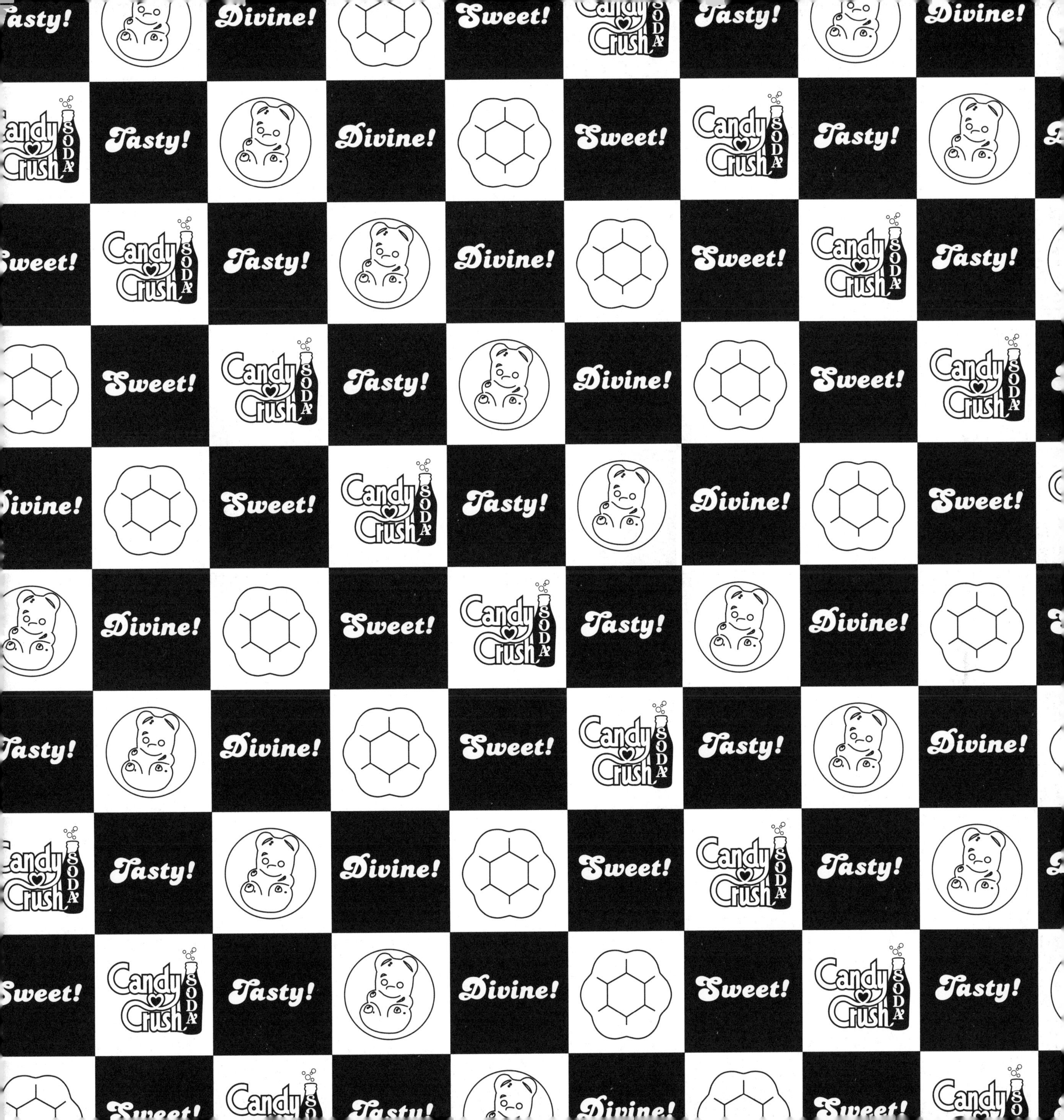
Tasty!
Divine!
Sweet!
Candy Crush SODA

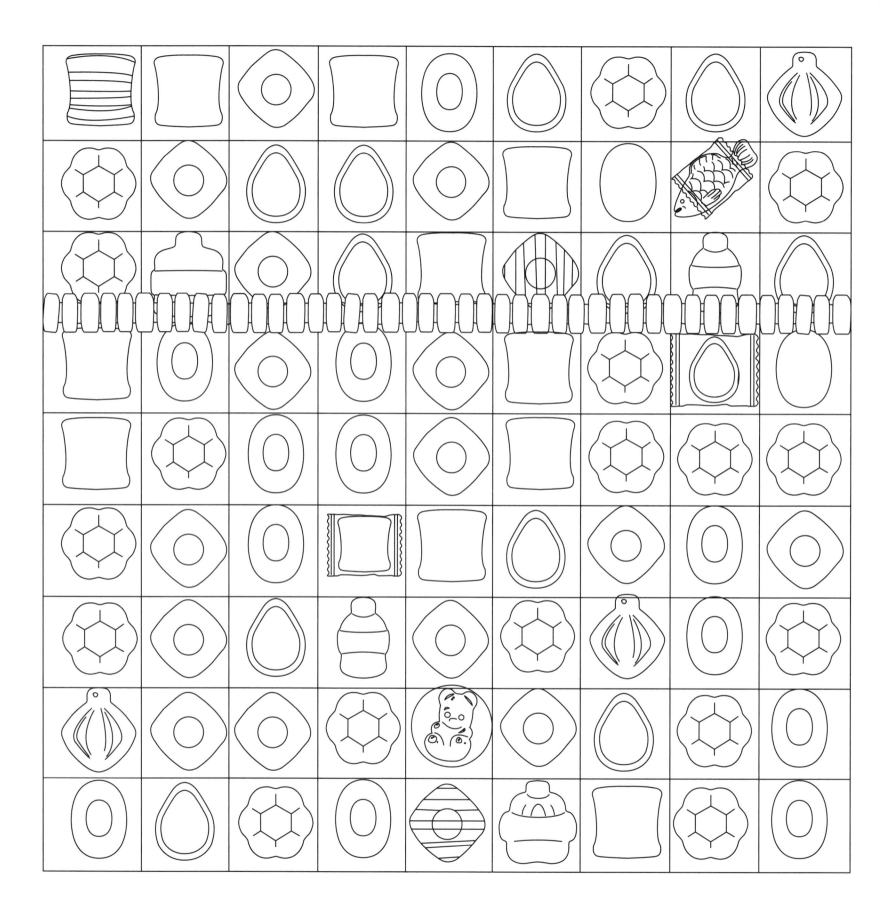

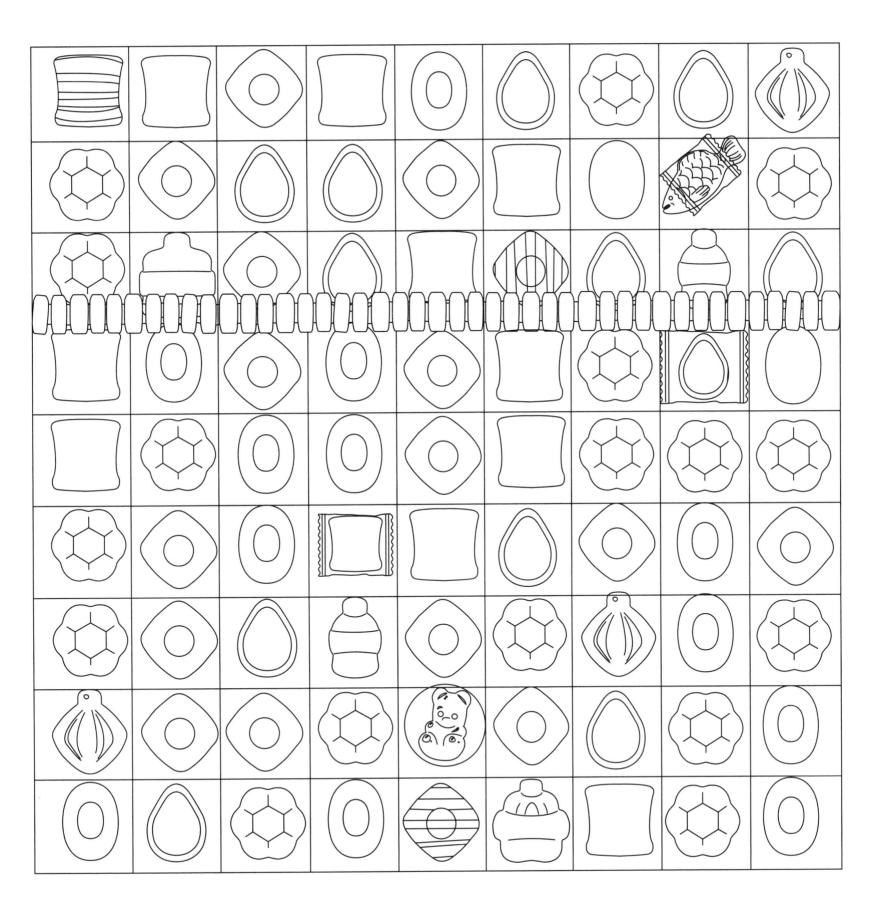

Tasty!

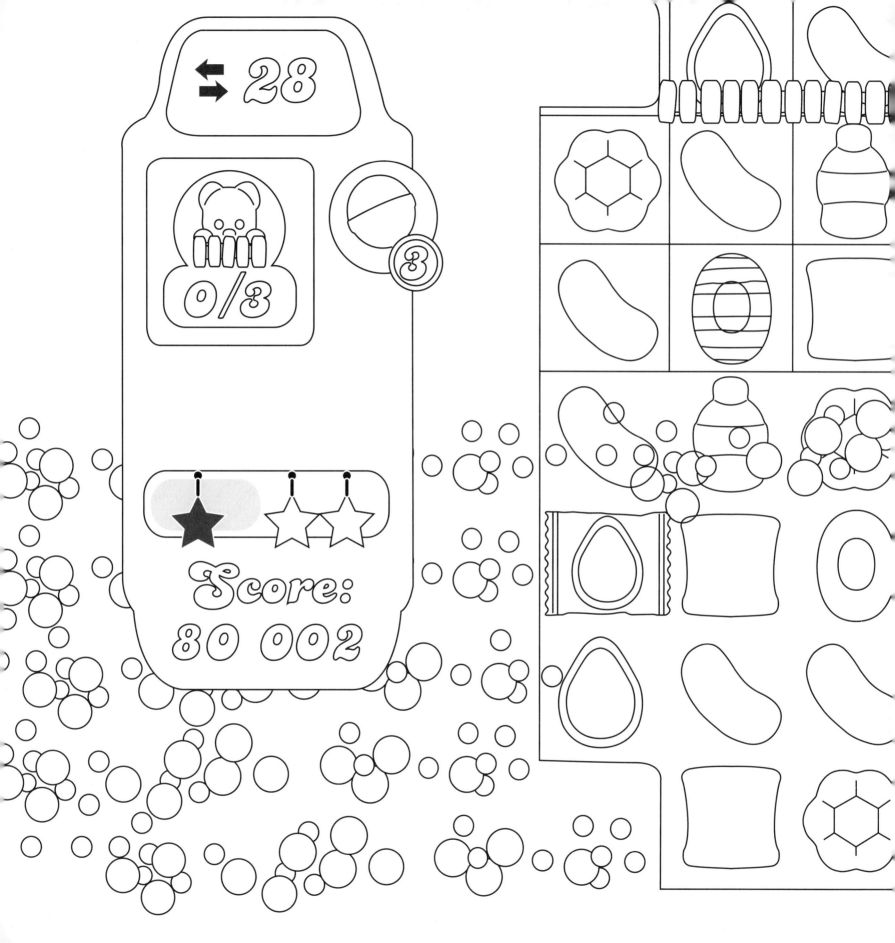

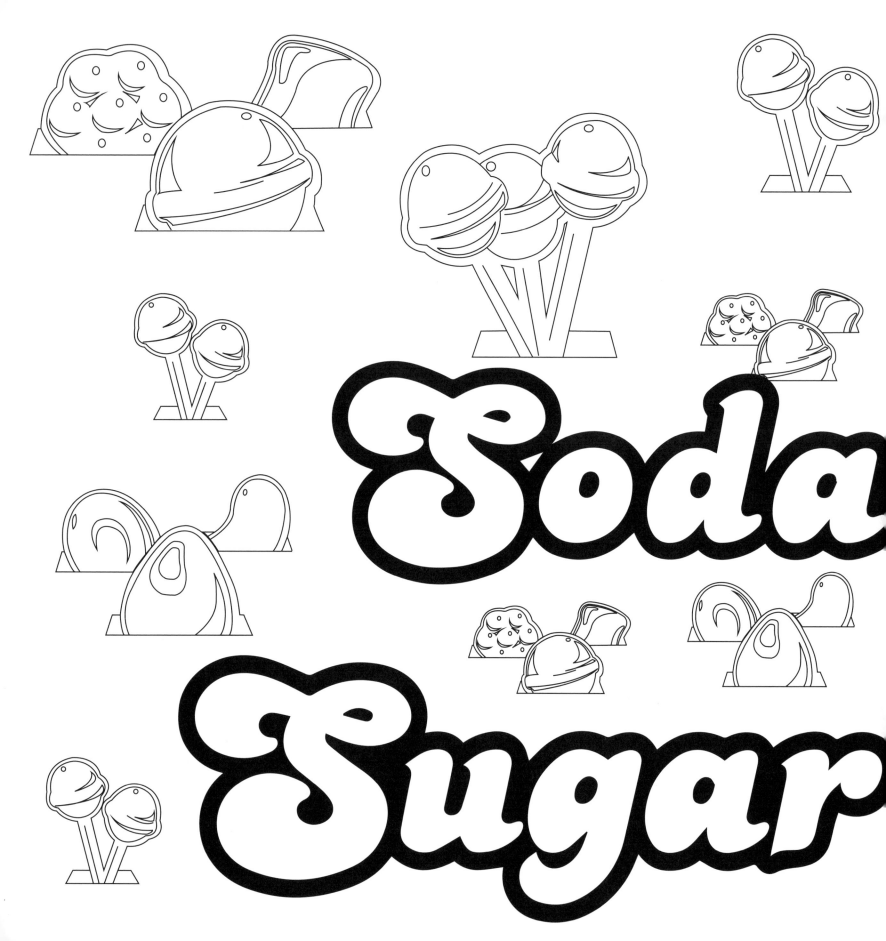

Make up your own

Sodalicious design!

Freestyle!

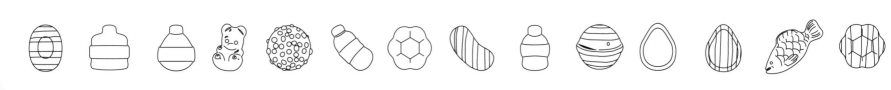

Crush!

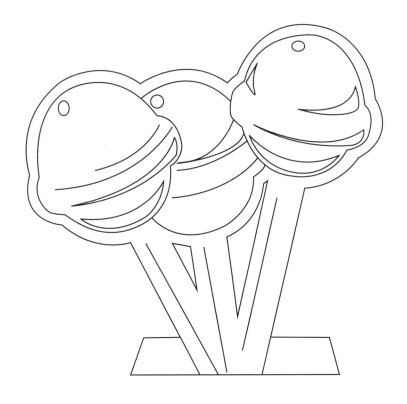